Good For You Cookies!

Jane Marsh Dieckmann

Edited by Andrea Chesman

The Crossing Press, Freedom, California 95019

This book is for Dick—
for more reasons than I could possibly say.

Library of Congress Cataloging-in-Publication Data

Dieckmann, Jane M.
   Good for you cookies! / Jane Marsh Dieckmann.
      p.   cm.
   Includes index.
   ISBN 0-89594-252-6 : $19.95.   ISBN 0-89594-253-4 (pbk.) : $7.95
   1. Cookies. I. Title.
TX772.D54 1987
641.8'654--dc19
                                                        87-18930
                                                           CIP

Contents

1
ABOUT COOKIES

What would life be for us without cookies? They are surely an essential part of the American scene and a leading element in our cooking tradition from the very beginning of our country's history. I doubt that any of us could envisage a world without them—they are the most popular between meal snack of all. They come crumbly and chewy, crisp and crunchy, thick and thin. They are easy to pick up and certainly are portable.

Cookies are the perfect accompaniment to ice cream and to fresh, canned, or thawed frozen fruit; they are the backbone of the afternoon tea, the punch party, the dessert buffet. Where would the fundraising bake sale be without them? Or Christmas?

We all love cookies. And what memories they conjure up! For many of us, our first real cooking experience was the baking of cookies, complete with the dollop of raw dough surreptitiously licked from our fingers and the freshly baked delights sneaked from the tray. We all can remember creeping up to bed with a good book, or sitting out under the tree, or settling down in front of the television or the radio or the record player—with a handful of cookies. For lots of us such memories are very fresh.

A cookie is defined as a small, flat, sweet cake eaten as a snack or with other desserts. The word comes from the Dutch *koekje*, meaning little cake, and first appears in print in 1703. In Britain the word isn't used much—the British eat "biscuits" —the French refer to cookies as "dry cakes," and the Germans usually give their cookies special names based on origin, ingredients, or shape—such as *Lebkuchen* or *Zimtsterne* (love cakes or cinnamon stars). But for us Americans, cookies are cookies and have been a favorite food ever since their introduction by the early Dutch settlers in the New World.

There are many different kinds of cookies. The early cookies were generally rolled and cut in shapes, and thus were crisp and short. Sometime in the past one hundred years, someone—who surely deserves a medal and our eternal thanks—invented drop cookies, which are irregularly round and quick to make and bake, as they require no rolling and cutting. Also let us give a medal to the person who came up with bar cookies, especially brownies, which will always vie in popularity with the famous and forever delicious chocolate chip or Toll House cookie. And there are cookies that can be chilled and sliced from a roll, put through a fancy food press, and even made without any baking.

In the past few years the ever-popular cookie has become even more so and is appearing everywhere. Today there are entire aisles in the supermarket stacked with cookies, shops that sell only cookies, huge meal-sized cookies, tiny cookies in decorative tins, rich and fancy cookies, plain cookies, even cookies in ice cream.

So that is the good news. Unfortunately, however, the bad news is that a lot of really dreadful cookies are out there being consumed. Many are bad for you because they are loaded with chemicals and preservatives and artificial ingredients as well as an overwhelming amount of bleached flour and refined sugar. And most have simply too many empty calories. In addition many don't taste very good—they lack an interesting texture, a lively flavor, an appealing combination of ingredients. Since we are going to eat cookies to the ends of our lives, it is really too bad to waste time and calories on anything but the very best—for taste and food value.

In this book you will find recipes for cookies that are good for you—highly nutritious and simply delicious. And these cookies are more interesting and flavorful than the conventional and rather dull butter-and-sugar cookie. Their food value has been boosted by the addition of substantial ingredients—whole grains, high-fiber breakfast cereals, nonfat dry milk, blackstrap molasses, fruit juices, fruits, nuts, and seeds—rich in vitamins and minerals and containing important body-building nutrients. White sugar and white flour, both of which are highly refined—almost purified—ingredients, have been kept to a minimum. Most recipes in this book call for unrefined and unprocessed sweeteners—honey, blackstrap molasses, pure maple syrup. Although butter, a saturated fat, is not considered to be very good for us, most recipes contain some butter, simply because its flavor is so special and essential to many truly delicious cookies. The significant issue here is not that you use butter or oil (or even white sugar for that matter) in your cookies, but that you use these ingredients with moderation and that—even more important—you balance and boost them with other ingredients of high nutrient value.

The cookies here represent the best of our tradition—all shapes and sizes, various flavors and textures, differing appeals and uses. In almost every case they should make you feel you have eaten something really good—for your palate to be sure, but also for your general physical well-being and health. Cookies that are good for you don't have to taste like sawdust or have all the allure of corrugated cardboard. On the contrary, they can be crunchy, chewy, substantial—the special delicious treat they should be.

Ingredients

The major elements in cookie making are fairly limited and easy to obtain. We are talking mainly about such basic staples as flour, sugar, and butter. But I want to make some suggestions here about a wider range of ingredients and to offer some tips on substitutions for more interesting flavor and texture as well as higher food value.

Flours. White flour means unbleached all-purpose flour. Be sure that you use enriched flour. Most of the recipes in this book contain some white flour, but usually a whole grain flour is the main ingredient. The whole grain flours contain both the germ and the bran of the grain, which are a major source of B vitamins and vitamin E, as well as a good source of protein, calcium, and iron. The bran (the outer layers of the grain) also contains noncaloric cellulose fiber, or roughage. Most of these elements have been processed out in the milling of all-purpose white flour; some vitamins and minerals are added back in enriched white flour, but none of the natural fiber has been replaced.

I have found that whole wheat pastry flour, especially when it is combined with wheat germ, makes delicious and light cookies. Don't hesitate to substitute it for white flour in your own favorite recipes.

Rye flour (dark rye flour, that is, which contains the bran and the germ) and oat flour (which you can make yourself by whirling rolled oats in your blender until they are powdered) are excellent additions to cookie doughs. Soy flour adds significant protein, but it has a distinctive flavor (which many people don't like) and should be used sparingly.

Grains and Cereals. As we all know, rolled oats — especially beneficial as they have the highest protein of the commonly eaten grains — are essential to many cookie recipes. Try some rolled wheat for a pleasant change. Wheat germ makes a wonderful addition to cookies, as it adds flavor, lightness, and crunch, not to mention protein, vitamin E, and B vitamins. Adding bran will not add much in the way of flavor to your cookies, but it will add fiber. Many doctors today are prescribing oat bran for lowering cholesterol. A good way to consume it is in cookies. For you to use it effectively, however, make sure the recipe contains no butter, nuts, or coconut.

I use a lot of breakfast cereals in my cookies — in addition to rolled oats and wheat, there are the puffed and/or crunchy wheat, rice, corn, and millet cereals. Many of these are available in health food stores in unrefined whole grain versions. I find crisp brown rice cereal to be especially good for baking, as are the many good commercial ready-to-eat cold cereal varieties. A bewildering number of corn, bran, rice, oat, and wheat flakes are stocked in the supermarket. Do use the ones you like yourself, but read the ingredient panels before you buy: look for whole grains, little salt, low or no sugar, and absolutely no additives. I use a lot of Kellogg's All-Bran, Nutri-Grain, and Special K, and Post's Grape-Nuts. These cereals are enriched with added vitamins and minerals. In fact, a serving of some of these cereals provides the recommended dietary allowances of certain vitamins and minerals. In addition, the commercial granolas—although many are overly sweet—make good cookies; you can always use less sweetening in the recipe, and taste before baking.

Shortening. I use salted butter in these recipes, but there is little additional salt in my cookies. I do include some margarine and unsaturated vegetable oil, of which safflower and sunflower are the best.

Sweeteners and Liquids. There isn't much white sugar in my baking. I prefer the taste of brown sugar and really like cookies that are less sweet anyway. Most cookie recipes that you find in cookbooks have far too much sugar in them. I find honey to be a superb sweetener in cookies, especially in the soft, chewy varieties. It is true that the nutritional advantage of honey over sugar is only a negligible amount of minerals, but the flavor is delicious and because of honey's very sweet taste, you need much less of it. Molasses has a special taste and is a good source of iron and calcium as well; besides, nothing else will do in dark spice cookies. Do not forget maple syrup; it is more expensive but it adds a distinctive flavor to the very special cookie.

Fruit juices and fruit juice concentrates add flavor, sweetness, and liquid to your cookies along with minerals and vitamins, especially A and C. The addition of milk, cream (sweet or sour), cream or farmer cheese, and yogurt will provide protein and calcium as well as flavor. And dry milk will provide the same protein and calcium boost without adding liquid.

Fruits, Nuts, Seeds. My favorite cookies have some sort of fruit in them, which adds not only flavor and fiber, but valuable nutrients. I love raisins and dates in cookies; not only is there added sweetness, but raisins are rich in iron and vitamin C and dates in potassium, so important to proper muscle function. Pineapple and cranberries are good sources of vitamin A, while the citrus fruits with their rinds and candied peels provide both vitamins A and C. Apricots and prunes give us significant amounts of vitamin A, calcium, potassium, and iron, while figs add potassium and calcium. Make sure the dried fruits are cut in small pieces. Chopped raw apples, applesauce, and mashed bananas—all good sources of potassium—are delicious in cookies.

Often the essential flavor of a cookie depends on nuts, and adding nuts to cookies is yet another way to boost the food value. All the nuts—as well as peanuts, which are really a vegetable—are rich in the B vitamins and minerals and are good sources— peanuts especially—of protein and calcium. And coconut adds phosphorous. The nuts do add fat to cookies, though. One delicious alternative is soy grits, which give a nutty flavor and the bonus of protein and some calcium. You can substitute them for nuts in most recipes.

And don't neglect the seeds. Rich in flavor, nutrition, and crunch, sunflower, sesame, and poppy seeds also add protein, vitamin A, phosphorus, and iron.

The message here is to consider these ingredients as ways to enhance the food value and good taste of the cookies you like best to make. Do feel free to experiment and to try unusual combinations. A great advantage of making cookies is that it is almost impossible to come up with a bad result.

Equipment

You don't need very much to make good cookies. I use an electric mixer—and have for many, many years. One of my daughters just wades in with her hands, another time-tested method. If you don't use an electric mixer, it is useful to have something to beat the eggs with—a beater, whisk, or fork—and a stout, preferably large, mixing spoon. You will also need measuring spoons and cups (and please use level measures, the results will be more reliable), and a set of mixing bowls.

As for baking pans and cookie sheets, you will need square pans, in both 8-inch and 9-inch sizes, and rectangular pans, the usual sizes being 13 inches by 9 inches and 14 inches by 10 inches. Traditional baking sheets are rectangular and flat.

As for greasing the pans, I almost never do it any more. Most baking sheets are treated now, and if you follow the manufacturer's directions for seasoning them before using the first time, there should be no need for you to grease yours either. Most cookies contain enough shortening to prevent sticking, and when I have finished a batch, I wipe the sheet with a paper towel. The grease remaining on the sheet from the

cookies makes a useful light coating for the next round. The square and rectangular pans, especially if they are Teflon coated, need only the lightest wiping. If the cookies or bars contain no shortening at all, however, a light greasing will prevent sticking. Here is another case where experimentation will tell you what to do. If greasing the baking sheets or pans doesn't seem to be needed, then why bother?

Making Cookies

Among the many wonderful things about cookies is that they are so easily made. Here are a few general rules to make the job even easier.

Bake one sheet or pan of cookies at a time and use the center rack of the oven. Make sure the oven is preheated to the temperature you want before you put the cookies in. And keep an eye on them. Check cookies when the minimum baking time is up. Cookies can always be baked more, but looking at them too late is, well, too bad.

Have at least two cookie sheets on hand, so that one sheet can be baking while you are filling the other. When you take cookies from the oven, remove them at once to a wire rack or a tray covered with waxed paper. Don't pile them on top of one another.

Have all your ingredients at room temperature. I always take eggs, butter, and any dairy products out of the refrigerator at least an hour before preparation time. Most cookie recipes follow the same general method: the shortening and sweetening are creamed together, then the eggs are beaten in, and the dry ingredients are added last, sometimes in alternation with liquids. Be sure that the creaming is done thoroughly and that the eggs are beaten in well. After the dry ingredients are added, generally it is best to treat the dough gently—this will make for crisper and more tender cookies. While you are waiting for your refrigerated ingredients to come to room temperature, you can measure the dry ingredients and cut or chop the fruits and nuts called for in the recipe. In other words, have everything assembled and ready to go at the time you start the actual mixing of the dough.

Storing Cookies

Empty coffee cans, shortening tins, or even large plastic containers work well for storage. Line the bottom of the container with waxed paper or clear storage wrap; if you like, you can also use more between each layer of cookies. Always store crisp and soft cookies in separate containers.

Soft Cookies. Store in a container with a tight-fitting lid. A slice of apple or soft bread in the container will help keep the cookies moist. Be sure to replace it often to prevent mold.

Crisp Cookies. Store airtight and in a cool place. Keep them in the refrigerator, if there is space. At Christmastime a good place is the porch, where for most of us it is very cold indeed. If stored very cold, most crisp cookies keep well for weeks. Should they get soft, reheating in a 300° F. oven for a few minutes will restore crispness.

Bar Cookies. You can store them right in the pan, but I prefer to take them out, put them in a cookie tin, and store them in a cool place.

Freezing Cookies

Most cookies can be frozen either before or after baking. All refrigerator cookie dough can be frozen for a long time, and often can be taken from the freezer and sliced right away. Dough for rolled cookies should stand at room temperature for about ten minutes before you roll it out. Dough that is very cold may be crumbly, and often needs a slightly longer baking time. If you have any doubts, it is better to bake the cookies and then freeze them. Raw dough that is very soft or that has lots

of eggs in it will not freeze well.

Freezing baked cookies is simple, and what could be more useful than to be able to take a container of cookies from your freezer and have them ready in minutes? Most drop cookies thaw almost instantly; bar cookies need a little more time. Do be sure that cookies are completely cooled before you freeze them, and pack them carefully so that they do not break in the freezer.

Mailing Cookies

Select cookies—bar and soft drop cookies are good—that will hold up under the duress of the postal service. If you really want to do it right, wrap each cookie or bar separately in clear plastic wrap or aluminum foil, or wrap two together. Make sure the cookies are well protected in a solid tin and carefully packed to prevent crushing or jostling. The tin can then be placed securely in a heavy cardboard box, well surrounded with packing materials. Mark the package "Fragile" and "Perishable."

About Yields

One final note: I have not provided yields
for these recipes. So much depends on the
size of your spoon and how you heap it for
drop cookies, how large you cut your bars
or squares, how large you make your refrigerator cookie rolls and how thin you
slice them, how thinly you roll out your
cookie dough. The size of your cookies is
really up to you—and so, consequently, is
the yield.

2
DROP COOKIES

I would guess that drop cookies are the most popular and most frequently made of all cookies. They are fun and easy to make, and can come in any size you wish. Be sure to allow enough space between cookies on the baking sheet—about two inches—as they are inclined to spread out. The cookie dough is mostly easily dipped out with a teaspoon and pushed off onto the cookie sheet with your finger. Some people like to use two spoons. Dough that is fairly stiff can be rolled in balls between the palms of the hands and then flattened with a greased and floured flat-bottomed glass or measuring cup. This makes a neat round cookie, which can be spaced one inch apart. A friend of mine purchased a small ice cream scoop, which she uses for drop cookies, thus creating cookies of uniform size and shape. If you want your drop cookies in a particular form, you can shape them with a spoon and neaten up the rough edges. Most of us just drop them on the sheet and bake them as is.

The recipes in this section make cookies that range from the soft (in the beginning of the chapter) to the crisp. I placed the macaroons last. These also vary from soft to crisp. They stand by themselves as they contain no shortening.

Apple Drop Cookies

1 cup whole wheat pastry flour
½ cup rye flour
¼ cup white flour
1 teaspoon baking soda
¼ teaspoon salt
1 teaspoon cinnamon
½ teaspoon cloves
½ teaspoon allspice
½ teaspoon nutmeg
¼ cup wheat germ
1 cup finely chopped walnuts
1 cup raisins, chopped
1 cup finely chopped unpeeled red apple
¼ cup butter, at room temperature
¼ cup oil
¾ cup brown sugar
1 egg
¼ cup apple cider

These cookies have a distinct spicy fruit flavor and a good chewy texture. If you want, glaze them while they are still warm with Orange Glaze (page 111) or Honey Glaze (page 117).

Sift together the flours, baking soda, salt, and spices into a large bowl; stir in the wheat germ, walnuts, raisins, and apple.

Cream the butter with the oil, sugar, and egg until light and fluffy. Add the apple cider and beat until combined. Stir in the flour mixture and blend well.

Drop by the heaping teaspoon, 2 inches apart, onto lightly greased cookie sheets. Bake in a preheated 400° F. oven for 8 minutes or until golden brown.

Currant Drop Cookies

¼ cup butter, at room temperature
¼ cup margarine, at room temperature
¾ cup honey
3 egg yolks
1 teaspoon vanilla extract
½ teaspoon grated lemon rind
1 cup whole wheat pastry flour
1 cup white flour
1 teaspoon baking powder
¼ teaspoon salt
¼ cup rolled oats
¼ cup nonfat dry milk powder
¼ cup milk
1 cup currants, plumped

These cookies are soft and golden in color. They make a perfect accompaniment to a simple afternoon tea.

Cream together the butter, margarine, and honey until light. Beat in the egg yolks, vanilla, and lemon rind.

Sift together the flours, baking powder, and salt; then mix in the rolled oats and milk powder. Add these dry ingredients to the butter mixture alternately with the milk. Beat the batter until smooth and then stir in the currants (plump them by pouring boiling water over; let them stand a minute or two and then drain thoroughly).

Drop the batter by the teaspoon onto lightly greased cookie sheets. Bake in a preheated 350° F. oven for about 10 minutes.

Banana Date Drops

♡♡♡

1 cup whole wheat pastry flour
1 tablespoon low-fat soy flour
2 tablespoons oat bran
½ teaspoon baking soda
½ teaspoon salt
½ teaspoon nutmeg
½ cup chopped toasted sunflower seeds
1 medium-sized ripe banana
2 tablespoons orange juice concentrate
½ cup well-packed pitted dates
1 large egg
1 teaspoon vanilla extract

This is a soft cookie, rich in potassium from the bananas and dates. Here is a good place to try oat bran in your baking.

In a large mixing bowl, combine the flours, oat bran, baking soda, salt, nutmeg, and seeds. Mix well and set aside.

Mash the banana in the blender with the orange juice concentrate and then add the dates, egg, and vanilla. Process until the dates are chopped and the mixture is fairly smooth.

Pour the banana mixture into the dry ingredients and mix well.

Drop the dough by the teaspoon onto lightly greased cookie sheets, flattening and shaping with the back of the spoon. Bake in a preheated 350° F. oven for about 10 minutes. These cookies freeze well.

Oatmeal Saucers

⅓ cup butter, at room temperature
⅓ cup oil
½ cup honey
1 egg
¾ cup thick sweetened applesauce
1 tablespoon grated orange rind
1 tablespoon thawed orange juice
    concentrate
1 cup whole wheat pastry flour
½ cup white or oat flour
1½ teaspoons baking powder
½ teaspoon salt
1 cup rolled oats
¾ cup chopped walnuts

The combination of applesauce and oatmeal is one of the best in my view. If you wish, glaze these when cool with Orange Glaze (page 111).

Cream together the butter, oil, and honey until blended. Add the egg and mix well. Stir in the applesauce, orange rind, and orange juice.

Sift together the flours, baking powder, and salt; stir in the rolled oats and walnuts. Add to the creamed mixture.

Drop by the heaping teaspoon onto lightly greased cookie sheets. Bake in a preheated 400° F. oven for 12 minutes.

Variation

Fruitcake Cookies. Substitute brown sugar for the honey. Stir in 1 cup chopped mixed candied fruits and peels and 1 cup fresh cranberries, chopped.

Fruited Oatmeal Cookies

½ cup butter, at room temperature
¼ cup margarine, at room temperature
¼ cup oil
½ cup firmly packed brown sugar
½ cup honey
2 eggs
¼ cup yogurt, sour milk, or buttermilk
1 cup whole wheat pastry flour
½ cup white flour
1 teaspoon baking powder
1 teaspoon baking soda
1 teaspoon cinnamon
1 teaspoon nutmeg
½ teaspoon salt
3 cups rolled oats
¼ cup wheat germ
1½ cups fresh or frozen cranberries, chopped
½ cup chopped walnuts
Cran-Orange Glaze (page 112) (optional)

For a change of taste, try substituting ½ cup maple syrup for the honey.

Cream together the butter, margarine, oil, brown sugar, and honey until smooth. Beat in the eggs and yogurt.

Sift together the flours, baking powder, baking soda, spices, and salt. Add to the creamed mixture. Stir in the oats, wheat germ, cranberries, and nuts.

Drop 2 inches apart onto lightly greased cookie sheets and bake in a preheated 400° F. oven for about 10 minutes. If desired, frost while warm with Cran-Orange Glaze.

Variation

Cashew Date Treats. This is an exotic variation indeed. For the cranberries and walnuts, substitute 1 cup finely chopped dates, ½ cup chopped raisins, and 1 cup chopped raw cashews.

Spicy Fruit Drops

1 cup whole wheat pastry flour
¼ cup white flour
1 cup wheat germ
½ teaspoon baking soda
¼ teaspoon salt
1 teaspoon cinnamon
¼ teaspoon cloves
¼ teaspoon nutmeg
¼ cup butter, at room temperature
¼ cup margarine, at room temperature
½ cup brown sugar
2 eggs
¼ cup yogurt or sour milk
1 cup chopped dates
1 cup raisins
½ cup chopped walnuts
Orange Glaze (page 111) (optional)

Measure the flours, wheat germ, baking soda, salt, and spices into a bowl. Stir well to blend.

Cream the butter and margarine with the sugar and eggs. Add the dry ingredients alternately with the yogurt or sour milk. Stir in the dates, raisins, and nuts.

Drop by the level teaspoon onto lightly greased cookie sheets and bake in a preheated 350° F. oven for 15 to 18 minutes. If desired, glaze while warm with Orange Glaze.

Variation

Bran Drop Cookies. Use sour milk and increase the amount to ½ cup; substitute 1 cup All-Bran cereal for the wheat germ. Combine these two ingredients and let them stand for a minute or two before stirring them into the creamed mixture alternately with the dry ingredients.

Zucchini Cookies

½ cup honey
¼ cup oil
1 egg, beaten
1 cup grated, drained, and closely packed zucchini
⅔ cup whole wheat pastry flour
¼ cup white or oat flour
2 tablespoons wheat germ
2 tablespoons oat bran
½ teaspoon baking soda
½ teaspoon cinnamon
¼ teaspoon nutmeg
¼ teaspoon salt
½ teaspoon lemon juice

Here is a good way to get some vegetables into the children. These cookies are tender, slightly spicy, and have pretty green flecks from the zucchini.

Combine the honey and oil. Add the egg, then the zucchini.

In another bowl, mix together the dry ingredients and then add them to the zucchini mixture. Stir in the lemon juice.

Drop by the teaspoon onto lightly greased cookie sheets. Bake in a preheated 350° F. oven for 10 to 15 minutes.

Variation

Pumpkin Nut Cookies. Substitute 1 cup mashed cooked pumpkin for the zucchini and stir in ½ cup chopped walnuts.

Golden Cookies

2 eggs
½ cup molasses
⅓ cup oil
1 cup mashed cooked sweet potatoes or carrots
1 cup whole wheat pastry flour
⅓ cup wheat germ
2 tablespoons oat bran
1 tablespoon nutritional yeast
1 cup nonfat dry milk powder
½ teaspoon salt
¼ teaspoon cinnamon
¼ teaspoon nutmeg
¼ teaspoon allspice
¼ teaspoon ginger

These have a hearty yellow orange color. They make a very healthy Halloween treat, considering that both sweet potatoes and carrots are high in vitamin A, the nutritional yeast adds valuable B vitamins and iron, and the dry milk provides a protein and calcium boost. Raisins or dried currants make good jack-o'-lantern faces and add even more nutrients. These sure beat packaged candy!

Beat the eggs first, then blend in the molasses and oil. Add the remaining ingredients. The dough will be stiff; add some orange or white grape juice if it is too thick.

Drop by the teaspoon onto lightly greased cookie sheets. Bake in a preheated 350° F. oven until lightly browned, about 15 minutes.

Dark Molasses Cookies

¼ cup butter, at room temperature
¼ cup margarine, at room temperature
¼ cup oil
½ cup molasses
¼ cup brown sugar
2 eggs
2 cups whole wheat pastry flour
2 teaspoons baking soda
1 teaspoon cinnamon
1 teaspoon ginger
½ teaspoon cloves
¼ teaspoon salt
¼ cup wheat germ
White sugar

This is a classic recipe and one of the most popular soft cookies ever. Be careful not to overbake these, as they are really best when moist and chewy.

Cream together the butter, margarine, oil, molasses, and brown sugar until very smooth. Beat in the eggs until well blended.

Sift together the flour, baking soda, spices, and salt. Mix in the wheat germ. Stir into the creamed mixture. Chill the dough for several hours.

Roll the chilled dough into balls the size of walnuts. Dip the tops in a little white sugar and place top side up on lightly greased cookie sheets. Press down slightly. Bake in a preheated 375° F. oven for 10 minutes.

2 sheets = 28 cookies spread very little

German Chocolate Drops

2 cups whole wheat pastry flour
½ cup white flour
½ teaspoon baking powder
½ teaspoon baking soda
1 teaspoon cinnamon
½ teaspoon cloves
¼ teaspoon salt
½ cup wheat germ
2 squares unsweetened chocolate
¼ cup butter, at room temperature
¼ cup margarine, at room temperature
½ cup brown sugar
¼ cup molasses
2 eggs
1 cup plain yogurt
1 teaspoon vanilla extract

This is a variation on an old-fashioned traditional cookie. Try serving these with stewed cherries, orange sections, or tart lemon or orange sherbet.

Sift together the flours, baking powder, baking soda, spices, and salt. Stir in the wheat germ and set aside.

Melt the chocolate over very low heat, or over hot water. Set aside.

Cream together the butter, margarine, sugar, and molasses until well blended. Beat in the eggs until light and fluffy, about 3 minutes. Then stir in the yogurt, vanilla, flour mixture, and, finally, the chocolate. Chill the dough for an hour.

Drop by the heaping teaspoon, 2 inches apart, onto lightly greased cookie sheets. Bake in a preheated 375° F. oven about 10 minutes.

Yogurt Cookies

⟡♡♡⟐♡ ♡♡ ♡♡♡ ♡♡♡♡♡♡ ♡♡♡♡♡♡♡♡♡♡♡♡♡♡♡♡ ♡♡♡♡♡♡♡♡♡♡♡♡♡♡♡♡♡♡♡♡

⅓ cup honey or less
3 tablespoons oil
⅓ cup plain or flavored yogurt
1 tablespoon grated orange rind
1 teaspoon vanilla extract
2 eggs, well beaten
½ cup whole wheat pastry flour
½ cup crunchy dry cereal (crisp rice or wheat flakes)
¼ cup wheat germ
¼ cup rolled oats or 2 heaping tablespoons oat bran
½ cup seedless raisins

If you find yourself with some leftover flavored yogurt, here is a good way to use it up. Use less honey, however, to compensate for the additional sweetness.

Blend the honey and the oil. Mix in the yogurt, orange rind, vanilla, and eggs. Then stir in the dry ingredients and the raisins.

Drop by the teaspoon onto lightly greased cookie sheets and bake in a preheated 400° F. oven for 8 to 10 minutes, or until set.

Superman Peanut Butter Raisin Cookies

¼ cup butter, at room temperature
¼ cup oil
⅓ cup honey
⅓ cup brown sugar
½ cup peanut butter
1 egg
¼ cup milk
½ cup whole wheat pastry flour
½ cup white flour
⅓ cup rolled oats
¼ cup nonfat dry milk powder
½ teaspoon baking soda
1 teaspoon cinnamon
Dash salt
1 teaspoon vanilla extract
½ cup raisins

These cookies get their name from a brand of peanut butter that was popular for a while. They are hearty and are guaranteed to make everyone big and strong. Do use peanut butter that has not been sweetened and is without additives.

Cream together the butter, oil, honey, and brown sugar until very smooth. Blend in the peanut butter, then the egg and milk.

Combine the flours, oats, dry milk, baking soda, cinnamon, and salt and stir them into the batter. Finally add the vanilla and the raisins.

Drop by the heaping teaspoon onto lightly greased cookie sheets and bake in a preheated 375° F. oven for about 15 minutes.

Variations

Peanut Date Cookies. Omit the raisins and cinnamon from the recipe. Add one more egg to the batter, increase the honey to ½ cup, and use a total of 2 cups rolled oats. Stir in 1 cup chopped dates.

Peanut Chocolate Chip Cookies. Omit the raisins and cinnamon and stir in 1 cup chocolate chips.

Frosted Carrot Cookies

1 cup diced carrots
1 cup whole wheat pastry flour
2 teaspoons baking powder
¼ teaspoon salt
1 cup rolled oats
¼ cup butter, at room temperature
¼ cup margarine, at room temperature
½ cup brown sugar
¼ cup peanut butter
1 egg
1 teaspoon vanilla extract
Orange Glaze (page 111)

Here is a good treat for Halloween. These cookies are somewhat tender, but they are the right color and children love them. And those carrots are brimming with vitamin A.

Cook the carrots in boiling water until very tender. Drain and mash them well.

Combine the flour, baking powder, salt, and oats and set aside.

Cream together the butter, margarine, and sugar; then add the peanut butter and egg and beat until light. Stir in the mashed carrots and vanilla and finally the dry ingredients.

Drop by the teaspoon onto lightly greased cookie sheets. Bake in a preheated 350° F. oven for 20 minutes or until golden. Cool thoroughly.

Frost the tops with Orange Glaze and decorate with raisins or currants if desired.

Orange Coconut Drops

1 large egg
¼ cup oil
½ cup honey
Grated rind of 1 medium-sized orange
3 tablespoons fresh orange juice
¾ cup whole wheat pastry flour
¼ cup wheat germ
¼ teaspoon salt
1 cup flaked coconut

Beat the egg well and add the oil and honey. Add the grated orange rind and the orange juice (which you can squeeze from the same orange). Then stir in the flour, wheat germ, salt, and coconut; blend very well.

Drop by the heaping teaspoon onto lightly greased cookie sheets and bake in a preheated 350° F. oven for about 15 minutes or until lightly browned.

Variations

Date Nut Coconut Cookies. Stir in ½ cup rolled oats, 1 cup chopped dates, and ½ cup chopped walnuts or pecans.

Chocolate Orange Drops. Add 2 ounces bitter chocolate, finely chopped.

Kichlach

4 large eggs
2 tablespoons light brown sugar
1 tablespoon very soft butter
1 cup whole wheat pastry flour
½ cup white flour
½ cup wheat germ
2 tablespoons poppy seeds
½ teaspoon cinnamon
½ teaspoon white sugar

This is a light, rather spongy cookie, with a delicate cinnamon-sugar topping. The cookies will puff up while baking and then settle. Add in some finely chopped almonds, if you like.

Beat the eggs on high speed until thick and lemony. Slowly crumble in the brown sugar and beat until smooth. Then beat in the butter. Quickly stir in the flours, wheat germ, and poppy seeds.

Drop by the teaspoon, about 2 inches apart, onto greased lightly greased cookie sheets. Mix together the cinnamon and white sugar and sprinkle over the cookies. Bake in a preheated 425° F. oven for 12 minutes or until puffed and brown.

Sesame Oatmeal Crisps

½ cup honey
½ cup oil
1 large egg, beaten
2 tablespoons milk
1¼ cups rolled oats
1 cup whole wheat pastry flour
1 teaspoon cinnamon
¼ teaspoon salt
2 tablespoons wheat germ
2 tablespoons oat bran
¾ cup sesame seeds
½ cup finely chopped raisins

These cookies are another popular choice in my house. They are firm and crunchy, and hold up very well on picnics. They are also good for sending through the mail.

Blend the honey, oil, and egg. Stir in the milk and oats. Then mix in the remaining ingredients in the order given. The dough will be stiff. If it seems too stiff, add more milk.

Drop by the teaspoon onto lightly greased cookie sheets. Flatten with the bottom of a glass dipped in cold water. Bake in a preheated 375° F. oven about 10 minutes.

Vanilla Sugar Cookies

½ cup butter, at room temperature
¼ cup oil
½ cup brown sugar
⅓ cup honey
⅓ cup nonfat dry milk powder
1½ teaspoons vanilla extract
1 large egg
¾ cup whole wheat pastry flour
¾ cup white flour
2 teaspoons baking powder
¼ teaspoon salt
¾ cup wheat germ

Here is a basic recipe, enriched with whole wheat flour, wheat germ, and dry milk, and adaptable to almost endless variations. The recipe is for a drop cookie, but the dough can also go in a cookie press. The baking time is the same.

Cream together the butter, oil, brown sugar, and honey until fluffy. Then add the dry milk, vanilla, and egg; beat well. Sift together the flours, baking powder, and salt. Stir into the creamed mixture along with the wheat germ.

Drop by the heaping teaspoon onto lightly greased cookie sheets (or shape into balls and press to ¼-inch thickness with a glass that has been buttered on the bottom). Bake in a preheated 400° F. oven for 10 minutes, or until the edges are lightly browned. Watch them because they burn easily.

Variations

Dark Walnut Sugar Cookies. Substitute molasses for the honey; add 1 teaspoon cinnamon, ½ teaspoon nutmeg, and 1 cup finely chopped walnuts.

Raisin Sugar Cookies. Add 1 cup raisins.

Almond Coconut Cookies. Reduce the vanilla to 1 teaspoon; add 1 teaspoon almond extract, ½ cup flaked coconut, and ½ cup ground almonds.

Chocolate Chip and Nut Cookies. Add 1 cup chocolate chips and ½ cup finely chopped pecans, walnuts, cashews, or macadamia nuts.

Crunchy Cereal Cookies

♡◇♡◇◇♡◇♡◇♡◇◇♡◇♡◇♡◇♡◇◇♡◇♡◇♡◇♡◇♡◇♡◇◇♡◇♡◇♡◇◇♡◇♡◇♡◇◇♡◇♡◇◇♡◇♡◇♡◇◇♡◇♡

⅔ cup whole wheat pastry flour
1 teaspoon baking powder
Dash salt
¼ cup butter
¼ cup oil
⅓ cup honey
1 egg
1 teaspoon vanilla extract
¼ teaspoon almond extract
¼ cup nonfat dry milk powder
1½ cups Grape-Nuts, crisp rice cereal, or cereal flakes
¾ cup flaked coconut

You can make these cookies with the breakfast cereal of your choice. Any low-sugar cereal flakes work very well, such as Special K, Bran Flakes, Nutri-Grain, or Wheaties. If you use Grape-Nuts, the cookies will have a very pronounced crunch, something that many of us like very much.

Sift together the flour, baking powder, and salt. Set aside.

Cream together the butter, oil, and honey. Beat in the egg, vanilla, and almond extract. Stir in the sifted ingredients, then the dry milk, cereal, and coconut.

Drop by the teaspoon onto lightly greased cookie sheets. Bake in a preheated 350° F. oven for 8 to 10 minutes.

Honey Nut Crisps

½ cup butter, at room temperature
½ cup oil
½ cup brown sugar
1 cup honey
1 egg
1 teaspoon vanilla extract
2 cups whole wheat pastry flour
1 cup white flour
2 teaspoons baking powder
1 teaspoon cinnamon
½ teaspoon salt
2 cups finely chopped walnuts or pecans

This is one of the most elegant and delicious drop cookies of all. The flavor and texture are both delicate. Try almonds or filberts or hickory nuts for variety.

Cream together the butter and oil; add the brown sugar and cream again. Beat in the honey, egg, and vanilla.

Sift together the flours, baking powder, cinnamon, and salt. Fold into the creamed mixture. Stir in the nuts.

Drop by the teaspoon, about 2 inches apart, onto lightly greased cookie sheets. Bake in a preheated 350° F. oven for 10 to 12 minutes.

Oatmeal Coconut Cookies

2 large eggs
¼ cup oil
½ cup honey
1 teaspoon almond extract
1 cup nonfat dry milk powder
1 cup flaked coconut
2 cups rolled oats
Lemon Frosting (page 113) (optional)

The coconut makes these cookies particularly appealing. If you wish, add ½ cup finely chopped almonds and/or ¼ cup finely chopped candied orange peel to the dough.

Beat the eggs until light and then blend in the oil, honey, and almond extract. Add the dry milk and mix well. Then stir in the coconut and rolled oats and mix thoroughly.

Drop by the heaping teaspoon, about 2 inches apart, onto lightly greased cookie sheets. Bake in a preheated 325° F. oven for about 20 minutes. Do watch them carefully; they brown easily on the bottom. If desired, frost when cool with Lemon Frosting.

Peanut Butter Blossoms

¾ cup chunky peanut butter
¼ cup butter, at room temperature
½ cup honey
¼ cup dark brown sugar
1 egg
1 teaspoon vanilla extract
1 cup whole wheat pastry flour
½ cup white flour
1 teaspoon baking soda
¼ cup wheat germ
White sugar
Chocolate candy stars or kisses

If you leave off the chocolate "blossom," you have a classic peanut butter drop cookie, which you can crisscross with a fork to flatten and give it the traditional look.

Cream together the peanut butter, butter, honey, and brown sugar until very light and fluffy. Beat in the egg and vanilla.

Sift the flours and baking soda together and blend into the peanut butter mixture along with the wheat germ.

Shape the dough into balls, roll in white sugar, and place on lightly greased cookie sheets. Flatten slightly. Bake in a preheated 375° F. oven for 7 minutes. Remove from the oven and firmly press a candy star or kiss onto the top of each cookie so the cookies crack around the edge. Bake for 2 to 5 minutes more, or until lightly browned.

Maple Pecan Cookies

¼ cup butter, at room temperature
¾ cup maple syrup
1 egg
¾ cup whole wheat pastry flour
¼ cup wheat germ
1 cup nonfat dry milk powder
Freshly grated rind of ½ lemon
3 tablespoons fresh lemon juice
1 cup coarsely chopped pecans

The distinctive taste of maple syrup makes these cookies special. They are very good with a baked or boiled custard.

Cream the butter until light and blend in the maple syrup. Beat in the egg and then stir in the remaining ingredients in the order given.

Drop by the teaspoon, about 2 inches apart, onto lightly greased cookie sheets. Bake in a preheated 350° F. oven for 20 to 25 minutes.

Variations

Honey Pecan Cookies. Substitute honey for the maple syrup.

Honey Poppy Seed Cookies. Substitute honey for the maple syrup and 2 tablespoons poppy seeds for the chopped pecans.

All-Nut Cookies

1½ cups shelled filberts
½ cup walnut pieces
2 eggs
¼ cup honey
½ teaspoon vanilla extract
Dash salt

It is essential to use filberts in these cookies. Their distinctive taste is an uncontested asset. Try serving these with fresh or frozen red raspberries, strawberries, or apricots.

Grind the nuts into a fine flour and pour into a mixing bowl. Beat the eggs well and blend in the honey. Then pour this mixture into the ground nuts along with the vanilla and salt. Blend thoroughly.

Spoon by the tablespoon onto lightly greased cookie sheets. These cookies will spread while baking, so give them room. Bake in a preheated 325° F. oven for about 30 minutes, or until firm on top and browning on the bottom.

Corn Flake Macaroons

2 egg whites, at room temperature
½ cup brown sugar
1 cup flaked coconut
2 cups corn flakes, slightly crushed
½ cup chopped walnuts
½ teaspoon vanilla extract

Macaroons are the best use I know for left-over egg whites. They also have the advantage of not requiring any shortening.

Beat the egg whites at the highest speed with an electric mixer until very stiff. Gradually add the sugar while beating all the time. Then fold in the remaining ingredients by hand.

Drop by the teaspoon onto well-greased cookie sheets. Bake in a preheated 350° F. oven until delicately browned, about 12 to 15 minutes.

Variations

Cereal Flake Macaroons. Substitute wheat or bran flakes for the corn flakes.

Almond Macaroons. Substitute ½ cup ground almonds for the walnuts and almond extract for the vanilla.

Lemon Macaroons. Substitute ½ cup ground almonds for the walnuts and 2 tablespoons lemon juice for the vanilla. Stir in 2 tablespoons grated lemon rind.

Chocolate Chip Macaroons. Add ½ cup finely chopped chocolate chips before baking.

Maple Granola Macaroons

2 egg whites, at room temperature
½ cup maple granules or maple sugar
2 cups granola
½ cup crisp brown rice cereal
½ cup flaked coconut
1 teaspoon vanilla extract

The combination of the maple flavor and the crunch of the granola make these macaroons scrumptious.

Beat the egg whites at highest speed in an electric mixer until stiff. Gradually add the maple granules and continue beating until very stiff and glossy. Add the remaining ingredients gently by hand and mix thoroughly.

Drop by the teaspoon onto well-greased cookie sheets. Bake in a preheated 350° F. oven for 10 to 12 minutes. Allow to cool for several minutes before removing from the cookie sheet.

3

BARS AND SQUARES

Here are cookies with a rich cakelike texture. They are by far the quickest to make and, for a bonus, they store and ship well. They are made by pouring the batter into a lightly greased baking pan; after baking they are cut in bars or squares, either warm or when cooled. Best known and most popular of the bar cookies are brownies, clearly an important element of our tradition. Here you will find other recipes as well, many of which deserve a wider reputation and consumption.

You can store bar cookies right in the baking pan, tightly covered with aluminum foil or plastic wrap. I prefer to remove them and store them in a tin or tightly wrapped in the freezer.

A ruler is useful for marking off even squares or bars.

Saucepan Brownies

½ cup whole wheat pastry flour
¼ cup white flour
½ teaspoon baking powder
¼ teaspoon baking soda
¼ teaspoon salt
3 tablespoons butter
2 tablespoons margarine
⅓ cup honey
2 tablespoons orange juice concentrate
1 cup chocolate chips
1 teaspoon vanilla extract
2 eggs
½ cup granola
½ cup flaked coconut

This recipe has several bonuses: granola, coconut, orange juice, and whole wheat flour which provide the fiber and vitamin boost of whole grains and citrus fruit. As you make these brownies in one pan, you save time in preparation and cleanup.

Sift together the flours, baking powder, baking soda, and salt. Set aside.

Combine the butter, margarine, honey, and orange juice concentrate in a large saucepan. Bring to a boil over moderate heat, stirring constantly. Remove from the heat and stir in the chocolate chips. Then add the vanilla. Add the eggs and beat well. Stir in the dry ingredients, granola, and coconut.

Spread in a lightly greased 9-inch square pan. Bake in a preheated 325° F. oven for 25 to 30 minutes. Cut into squares while warm.

Applesauce Fudge Squares

2 squares baking chocolate
¼ cup butter
¼ cup oil
2 eggs, beaten
½ cup molasses or dark honey
1 teaspoon vanilla extract
⅔ cup thick sweetened applesauce
¼ cup nonfat dry milk powder
¼ cup wheat germ
½ cup whole wheat pastry flour
¼ cup white flour
½ teaspoon baking powder
¼ teaspoon baking soda
¼ teaspoon salt

These moist, cakelike squares make a delicious after-school snack with cold milk. Like the Saucepan Brownies, they too have the one-pan advantage.

In a large saucepan, heat the chocolate with the butter and oil over very low heat until it is just melted. Add the eggs and blend them well. Stir in the molasses, vanilla, and applesauce. Then blend in the dry milk and wheat germ.

Sift together the remaining dry ingredients. Stir them in last.

Pour into an ungreased 9-inch square pan. Bake in a preheated 350° F. oven for 35 to 40 minutes. Cool and cut into squares.

Carob Banana Bars

1 cup carob chips
2 tablespoons margarine
½ cup whole wheat pastry flour
½ cup white flour
½ teaspoon baking powder
½ teaspoon baking soda
½ teaspoon salt
½ teaspoon cinnamon
¼ cup butter, at room temperature
¼ cup brown sugar
¼ cup molasses
¼ cup dry milk powder
1 cup mashed ripe bananas (3 medium-sized bananas)
1 egg
¼ cup milk
1 cup All-Bran cereal
1 cup chopped walnuts

These moist bars provide potassium from the banana, iron from the molasses, protein from the dry milk, and fiber from the cereal. They also provide a delicious chocolate-free option.

Melt the carob chips and the margarine over very low heat. Set aside.

Sift together the flours, baking powder, baking soda, salt, and cinnamon. Set aside.

Cream together the butter, brown sugar, molasses, and dry milk. Beat in the bananas, egg, milk, cereal, and cooled melted carob chips. Add the sifted ingredients and nuts. Mix until combined.

Spread the mixture in a well-greased 13-inch by 9-inch baking pan. Bake in a preheated 350° F. oven for about 25 minutes. Cool and cut into bars.

Apple Brownies

♢◇♡♢♡♢◇♡♢♡♢◇♡♢♡◇♢♡♢◇♡♢♡♢◇♡♢♡♢◇♡♢♡♢◇♡♢♡◇♢♡♢◇♡♢♡♢◇♡♢♡♢◇♡♢♡♢◇♡♢♡◇♢♡♢◇♡♢♡♢◇♡

¼ **cup margarine, at room temperature**
¼ **cup oil**
¼ **teaspoon salt**
1 egg, beaten
¾ **cup honey**
¼ **cup nonfat dry milk powder**
3 medium-size apples, pared and diced,
   or ½ cup thick, lightly sweetened
   applesauce
½ **cup chopped walnuts**
1 cup whole wheat pastry flour
½ **teaspoon baking powder**
½ **teaspoon baking soda**
½ **teaspoon cinnamon**

These easy-to-make squares are very moist, so keep them refrigerated or freeze them soon after baking.

Cream the margarine and oil with the salt; add the egg, honey, and dry milk. Beat well. Stir in the apples and nuts, then the dry ingredients, mixing well.

Pour into a lightly greased 8-inch square pan. Bake in a preheated 350° F. oven for about 40 minutes. Cool and cut into squares.

Date Brownies

♡▷♡♡♡▷♡▷♡♡▷♡▷♡♡♡♡♡▷♡♡♡♡♡♡♡♡▷♡♡♡▷♡♡♡♡♡♡▷♡♡♡♡♡▷♡♡♡♡♡▷♡♡♡▷♡♡♡♡♡♡♡

2 eggs
½ cup brown sugar
2 tablespoons honey
½ cup whole wheat pastry flour
1⅔ cups graham cracker crumbs
¼ cup oil
½ teaspoon vanilla extract
1½ cups chopped dates
½ cup chopped walnuts
¼ cup orange juice

This may seem an unusual recipe, but do try it. Dates and orange juice are a delicious — and potassium rich — combination.

Beat the eggs until light. Blend in the brown sugar and honey and beat until smooth. Stir in the flour and crumbs, and then the remaining ingredients in the order given.

Spread the mixture evenly in a lightly greased 8-inch square pan. Bake in a preheated 350° F. oven for 25 to 30 minutes. While still warm, cut into 20 bars.

Carrot Brownies

¼ cup butter
¼ cup margarine
⅓ cup molasses or dark honey
¼ cup brown sugar
1 cup whole wheat pastry flour
¼ cup white flour
¼ cup soy flour
2 teaspoons baking powder
¼ teaspoon salt
½ cup wheat germ
2 eggs
2 cups finely grated carrots
½ cup chopped walnuts
Cream Cheese Frosting (page 119)

These brownies are dark, chewy, and healthful bars—all that vitamin A, iron, and protein—good for afternoon snacks.

Melt the butter and margarine in a large saucepan. Add the molasses and brown sugar and stir until blended. Remove from the heat and cool slightly.

Sift together the flours, baking powder, and salt. Stir in the wheat germ and set aside.

Beat the eggs, one at a time, into the butter mixture. Then stir in the flour mixture. Add the carrots and walnuts and blend well.

Pour into 2 lightly greased 8-inch square pans (or one 14-inch by 10-inch pan) and bake in a preheated 350° F. oven for 25 to 30 minutes. Cool thoroughly and then spread with the Cream Cheese Frosting. Cut into bars.

Applesauce Spice Squares

1 cup whole wheat pastry flour
1 cup rye flour
1 teaspoon baking soda
1 teaspoon cinnamon
½ teaspoon nutmeg
¼ teaspoon cloves
Dash salt
¼ cup butter, at room temperature
¼ cup margarine, at room temperature
⅔ cup honey
1 egg
2 tablespoons nonfat dry milk powder
1½ cups thick sweetened applesauce or
   ¾ cup mashed cooked pumpkin and
   ¾ cup applesauce
½ cup dark raisins
½ cup golden raisins
½ cup soy grits or chopped walnuts

I make these squares very often. They are delicious with freshly made applesauce, mixed fresh fruit, or pumpkin custard. If you like a stronger spice flavor, increase the cinnamon to 2 teaspoons and the nutmeg to 1 teaspoon.

Sift together the flours, baking soda, spices, and salt and set aside.

Cream together the butter, margarine, and honey until fluffy. Beat in the egg. Stir the dry milk into the applesauce and add this to the creamed mixture alternately with the flour mixture. Blend well. Stir in the raisins and soy grits.

Spread in a lightly greased 14-inch by 10-inch pan. Bake in a preheated 350° F. oven for 25 minutes. Cool and cut into squares.

Pineapple Graham Squares

¼ **cup butter, at room temperature**
⅓ **cup brown sugar**
1 egg
½ **cup whole wheat flour**
½ **cup graham cracker crumbs**
1 can (8¾ ounces) crushed pineapple, well drained
½ **cup chopped walnuts**

These squares are moist, sweet, and easy to make, with a lovely taste of pineapple.

Cream the butter with the sugar until light and fluffy. Beat in the egg. Stir in the flour, crumbs, pineapple (be sure it is drained thoroughly), and walnuts.

Pour into a lightly greased 8-inch square pan. Bake in a preheated 350° F. oven for 30 to 35 minutes, or until lightly browned. Cool in the pan and cut into squares.

Energy Fruit Bars

2 eggs
2 tablespoons oil
1 teaspoon vanilla extract
3 tablespoons fruit juice
1 cup raisins
¼ cup chopped dates or dried apricots
½ cup honey or molasses
½ cup nonfat dry milk powder
½ cup wheat germ
⅓ cup whole wheat pastry flour
¼ cup bran
1 cup chopped nuts (walnuts, pecans, almonds)
½ cup sunflower seeds
½ cup sesame seeds

These bars are dark and loaded with nuts and seeds—such good sources of protein, calcium, and B vitamins.

Beat the eggs well and add in the oil, vanilla, and fruit juice. Stir in the remaining ingredients. The batter will be thick and rather sticky.

Spread the batter in a well-greased 9-inch square pan. Bake in a preheated 300° F. oven for 35 to 40 minutes or until firm. Cool and cut into squares.

Hermits

2 cups bran flake or Special K (slightly crushed) cereal
½ cup milk
1 cup whole wheat pastry flour
¼ cup wheat germ
¼ cup nonfat dry milk powder
½ teaspoon baking soda
½ teaspoon cinnamon
¼ teaspoon nutmeg
¼ teaspoon ginger
¼ cup butter, at room temperature
¼ cup oil
½ cup brown sugar
¼ cup molasses
2 eggs
1 teaspoon vanilla extract
½ cup coarsely chopped peanuts
1 cup seedless raisins
Butter Cream Frosting (page 115) or
  Butter Frosting (page 116) (optional)

This traditional cookie is dark and moist and spicy.

Combine the bran flakes and milk in a small bowl and let stand for about 2 minutes or until most of the milk is absorbed.

Combine the flour, wheat germ, dry milk, baking soda, and spices. Set aside.

Beat the butter, oil, brown sugar, and molasses until light and fluffy. Add the eggs, vanilla, and bran flakes and beat well. Stir in the dry ingredients until combined. Mix in the peanuts and raisins.

Spread the mixture in a lightly greased 14-inch by 10-inch pan and bake in a preheated 350° F. oven for 20 to 25 minutes. When cool, frost if desired with Butter Cream Frosting or Butter Frosting. Cut into bars.

Lemon-Glazed Date Bars

½ cup whole wheat pastry flour
½ cup white flour
½ cup oat flour
1½ teaspoons baking powder
¼ teaspoon salt
2 eggs
½ cup white sugar
¼ cup light honey
1 tablespoon melted butter
1 tablespoon hot water
2 cups finely chopped pitted dates
½ cup chopped walnuts or pecans
Lemon Glaze (page 113)

These bars are light in color and texture and make a fine accompaniment to afternoon tea. The combination of lemon and dates is delicious.

Sift the flours together with the baking powder and salt. Beat the eggs well, adding the sugar gradually; then beat in the honey. Blend in the butter and water, then the dates and nuts, and finally the flour mixture, gradually, mixing thoroughly.

Spread the mixture into 2 well-greased 8-inch square pans and bake in a preheated 325° F. oven for 30 to 35 minutes. Cool thoroughly. Spread the tops with Lemon Glaze. When it has set, cut into bars.

Oatmeal Date Bars

Filling

4 cups chopped dates
⅓ cup honey
¾ cup water
¼ cup lemon juice
½ cup chopped walnuts

Crust

1 cup whole wheat pastry flour
¼ cup white flour
¼ cup wheat germ
½ teaspoon baking soda
¼ teaspoon salt
½ cup butter, at room temperature
¼ cup oil
¾ cup brown sugar
1½ cups rolled oats

This classic is one of the rare good-for-you cookies that has been around for a long time. The bars are crumbly and crunchy with a delicious soft filling. Try them and try the variations, all of which taste simply wonderful.

To make the filling, combine the dates, honey, and water in a saucepan. Stir over medium heat until thickened (about 5 minutes). Remove from the heat and stir in the lemon juice and walnuts. Set aside.

Combine the flours, wheat germ, baking soda, and salt. Cream the butter, oil, and sugar. Stir in the flour mixture and then the rolled oats. Mix well with your hands until crumbly.

Press half the mixture into a lightly greased 13-inch by 9-inch pan. Spread the filling over. Cover with the remaining crust. Press lightly with your hands. Bake in a preheated 375° F. oven for 30 minutes. Cut into bars while warm.

Variations

Apricot-Pineapple Bars. Instead of the date filling, use 2½ cups apricots, cooked and chopped, which you combine in a saucepan with ¾ cup honey, 3 slices chopped canned or fresh pineapple, and 3 tablespoons hot water. Simmer for about 10 minutes, or until thick. Cool and stir in ¾ cup chopped walnuts.

Cranberry Bars. Instead of the date filling, combine 1 can (16 ounces) whole cranberry sauce or about 2 cups homemade sauce, ½ cup raisins, and ½ teaspoon almond extract.

Fig Bars. Instead of the date filling, combine 2½ cups finely chopped figs, ⅓ cup honey, and ¾ cup water. Cook over medium heat until thick, stirring constantly. Cool and stir in 2 tablespoons grated orange rind and ¾ cup finely chopped walnuts.

Orange Raisin Squares

1 orange
1 cup raisins
2 tablespoons butter, at room
  temperature
2 tablespoons margarine, at room
  temperature
⅓ cup honey
¼ cup dark brown sugar
1 egg
1 cup whole wheat pastry flour
½ cup white flour
½ cup wheat germ
¼ cup nonfat dry milk powder
1 teaspoon baking soda
¼ teaspoon salt
½ cup sour milk or buttermilk
½ cup 10X sugar
2 tablespoons honey

These cakelike squares are very moist, with a pronounced orange fruit flavor. The whole orange and the raisins provide a high-fiber bonus, plus important amounts of vitamin A, calcium, and potassium. The squares taste much richer than they are in reality.

Remove the seeds and pith from the orange. Grind the orange together with the raisins and put the mixture through the grinder twice. It should be finely chopped. Save 2 tablespoons for the icing. If the fruit is still coarse, combine it with the sour milk and whirl it in the food processor.

Cream the butter, margarine, ⅓ cup honey, and brown sugar until well blended. Add the egg and beat well. Combine the dry ingredients and stir them in alternately with the sour milk and the fruit mixture. Mix everything well.

Spread the batter in a lightly greased 9-inch square pan and bake in a preheated 350° F. oven for 30 minutes. Meanwhile, make the icing by combining the reserved fruit mixture with the 10X sugar and the remaining 2 tablespoons honey. After taking the pan from the oven, spread the top while still hot with the icing. Cool thoroughly before cutting into squares.

Apricot Layer Squares

Crust

¼ **cup butter, at room temperature**
¼ **cup margarine, at room temperature**
¼ **cup brown sugar**
½ **cup whole wheat pastry flour**
¼ **cup white flour**
¼ **cup wheat germ**
¼ **teaspoon salt**

Apricot Layer

⅔ **cup dried apricots**
2 eggs
½ **cup brown sugar**
¼ **cup honey**
⅓ **cup white flour**
½ **teaspoon baking powder**
Pinch salt
½ **teaspoon vanilla extract**
½ **cup chopped walnuts**

These fruity layered squares are among the best bar cookies you can find. They come in many combinations, of which these— along with the following Festive Raisin Squares and Prune Squares—are outstanding examples. The general principle is the same—a shortbread type crust is baked first, then covered with a fruit combination and baked again.

To make the crust, cream together the butter, margarine, and brown sugar. Then mix in the flours, wheat germ, and salt until crumbly. Here is a good use for the food processor; just process briefly. Press this mixture into a lightly greased 8-inch square pan. Bake in a preheated 350° F. oven until lightly browned, about 20 minutes.

While the crust bakes, prepare the apricot layer. Cover the apricots with water and boil for 10 minutes. Drain, cool, and chop well. Then beat the eggs with the brown sugar and honey until light. Stir in the flour, baking powder, and salt; then mix in the vanilla, walnuts, and chopped apricots. Spread over the prebaked crust, return to the oven, and bake for 30 minutes longer. Cool in the pan and cut into squares or bars.

Festive Raisin Squares

Crust

**Follow the directions for the crust on
page 64**

Raisin Layer

2 eggs
½ cup brown sugar
¼ cup honey
1 teaspoon vanilla extract
Pinch salt
1 tablespoon whole wheat pastry flour
1 tablespoon white flour
½ teaspoon baking powder
1 cup chopped raisins
¾ cup chopped pecans
¾ cup flaked coconut

*The combination of raisins, nuts, and co-
conut make especially rich and scrumptious cookies. Do use seeded raisins if you
can get them.*

Prepare the crust and pat it into a lightly
greased 8-inch square pan. Bake in a preheated 350° F. oven for 15 minutes.

To make the raisin layer, beat the eggs
well with the brown sugar and honey.
Blend in the remaining ingredients in the
order given. Spread over the prebaked
crust, reduce the oven temperature to 325°
F., and bake for 35 minutes, or until firm.
Cool and cut into squares.

Prune Squares

Crust

Follow the directions for the crust on page 64

Prune Layer

2 eggs
½ cup brown sugar
½ teaspoon vanilla extract
½ teaspoon baking powder
¼ teaspoon salt
1 tablespoon wheat germ
¾ teaspoon ground coriander or cinnamon
1 cup finely chopped pitted dried prunes

Here is a wonderful way to feed prunes (rich in fiber, vitamin A, and iron) to the children. These make an especially good snack for after school.

Prepare the crust and pat it into a lightly greased 8-inch square pan. Bake in a preheated 350° F. oven for 15 minutes.

To make the prune layer, beat the eggs, brown sugar, and vanilla until well blended. Stir in the remaining ingredients in the order given. Spread over the prebaked crust and bake for 30 minutes, or until the top is golden brown and firm. Cool and cut into squares.

Granola Dream Bars

Crust
Follow the directions for the crust on page 64, omitting the salt

Dream Layer
2 eggs
½ cup maple syrup or honey
1 teaspoon vanilla extract
1 tablespoon whole wheat pastry flour
1 teaspoon baking powder
¼ teaspoon salt
½ cup granola, preferably with fruits and nuts
½ cup coconut
½ cup raisins

These are ideal cookies for the boarding school or college care package. They are chewy and combine the whole grains of the granola with coconut and raisins. If you have maple syrup, do use it in this recipe.

Prepare the crust and pat it into a lightly greased 9-inch square pan or, for a thinner bar, a 13-inch by 9-inch pan. Bake in a preheated 350° F. oven for 15 minutes.

For the top layer, beat the eggs until light and then beat in the maple syrup and vanilla. Combine the flour, baking powder, and salt. Stir it into the egg mixture and then add the the remaining ingredients. Pour this mixture over the prebaked crust and bake for 20 minutes, or until lightly browned. Cool and cut into bars.

Cheesecake Squares

Crust

¼ cup butter, at room temperature
⅓ cup brown sugar
½ cup whole wheat pastry flour
½ cup white flour
½ cup finely ground pecans
¼ cup currant jelly

Filling

4 ounces cream cheese
½ cup cottage cheese or 4 ounces farmer cheese
2 tablespoons honey
1 egg
2 tablespoons lemon juice
½ teaspoon vanilla extract
Grated lemon rind

Here is an easy way to have a taste of cheesecake from time to time, plus a protein and calcium boost. Keep these squares refrigerated.

Cream the butter, add the brown sugar and flours, and mix until crumbly. Stir in the nuts. Reserve about ¾ cup of this mixture for a topping. Press the remainder into the bottom of a lightly greased 8-inch square pan. Bake in a preheated 350° F. oven for 15 minutes. Cool slightly and spread the currant jelly over the crust.

To make the filling, beat the cream cheese and cottage cheese together with the honey. Then beat in the remaining ingredients. Pour this over the prebaked crust and sprinkle the reserved crumb mixture over the top. Return to the oven and bake for 30 minutes. Cool, then cut into squares.

Lemon Bars

Crust

1 cup white flour
¼ cup whole wheat pastry flour
¼ cup rolled oats
2 tablespoons 10X sugar
¼ teaspoon salt
3 tablespoons butter, at room temperature
2 tablespoons margarine, at room temperature
3 tablespoons buttermilk or a little less whole milk

Lemon Layer

3 eggs
½ cup white sugar
¼ cup light honey
¼ cup lemon juice
3 tablespoons white flour
2 tablespoons nonfat dry milk powder
1 teaspoon baking powder
Dash salt
10X sugar (optional)

Combine the ingredients in the crust layer and pat into a lightly greased 9-inch square or 11-inch by 9-inch pan. Bake in a preheated 350° F. oven for 20 minutes.

Meanwhile, prepare the lemon layer by beating the eggs, sugar, and honey until thick. Then stir in the lemon juice, flour, dry milk, baking powder, and salt. Spread over the prebaked layer, return to the oven, and bake for 25 minutes more. If desired, sprinkle with 10X sugar while hot.

Maple Shortbread Bars

3 cups rolled oats (quick cooking, if possible)
½ cup brown sugar
½ cup white flour
½ teaspoon salt
½ cup butter
¼ cup margarine
1 teaspoon vanilla extract
2 cups flaked coconut
1 cup pure maple syrup
Dash salt

You can make the shortbread without the topping and have a simple and rich bar cookie, much beloved in the British Isles.

Combine the rolled oats, sugar, flour, and ½ teaspoon salt. Cut in the butter and margarine with a pastry blender or two knives, until the mixture resembles coarse corn meal. Stir in the vanilla and mix well. Press the mixture into a lightly greased 13-inch by 9-inch pan. Bake in a preheated 350° F. oven for 25 to 30 minutes or until golden.

Meanwhile, mix the coconut and maple syrup with a dash of salt in a saucepan. Cook gently and stir until the coconut absorbs the syrup. Spread this over the warm shortbread and bake for 10 minutes. Cut into bars while warm.

Honey Oatmeal Chews

¼ **cup butter, at room temperature**
¼ **cup margarine, at room temperature**
½ **cup clover or other light honey**
1 egg
1 teaspoon vanilla extract
¾ **cup whole wheat pastry flour**
½ **teaspoon baking powder**
½ **teaspoon baking soda**
¼ **teaspoon salt**
1 cup rolled oats
1 cup flaked coconut
½ **cup chopped dry-roasted peanuts or**
  toasted chopped almonds

Cream together the butter, margarine, and honey until light and fluffy. Add the egg and vanilla and beat well.

Sift together the flour, baking powder, baking soda, and salt; add to the creamed mixture. Then stir in the oats, coconut, and peanuts.

Spread in a lightly greased 13-inch by 9-inch pan. Bake in a preheated 325° F. oven for 25 to 30 minutes. When cool, cut into bars.

Variation

Molasses Oatmeal Chews. Substitute blackstrap molasses for the honey and ¼ cup wheat germ for ¼ cup of the whole wheat flour. Use walnuts instead of peanuts.

Chewy Squares

½ cup whole wheat pastry flour
2 tablespoons white flour
2 tablespoons soy flour
1 teaspoon baking powder
¼ teaspoon salt
2 tablespoons wheat germ
2 tablespoons oat bran
2 tablespoons nonfat dry milk powder
½ cup brown sugar
¼ cup honey or blackstrap molasses
¼ cup butter, melted
2 eggs, beaten
1 teaspoon vanilla extract
2 cups corn flakes, slightly crushed

This basic bar cookie has a distinct butterscotch or toffee flavor. You can use the cereal flakes you like best. Feel free to add some fruit and nuts and/or some coconut.

Sift the flours, baking powder, and salt into a large bowl. Stir in the wheat germ, oat bran, and dry milk. Then blend in the brown sugar, honey, melted butter, eggs, and vanilla. Add the corn flakes, reserving a few for the top.

Spread in a lightly greased 9-inch square pan. Sprinkle the remaining corn flakes over the top and press in firmly. Bake in a preheated 350° F. oven for 30 minutes. Cool completely. Cut into squares.

Congo Bars

1 cup whole wheat pastry flour
½ cup white flour
¼ cup soy flour
2½ teaspoons baking powder
½ teaspoon salt
1 cup rolled oats
¼ cup nonfat dry milk powder
⅓ cup butter
⅓ cup oil
1 cup brown sugar
½ cup dark honey
3 eggs
1 package (6 ounces) semisweet chocolate bits
1 cup chopped walnuts

Here is a bar version of the classic chocolate chip cookie. It's scrumptious and easily made in a saucepan.

Sift the flours together with the baking powder and salt. Stir in the rolled oats and dry milk and set aside.

Melt the butter in a large saucepan and stir in the oil, brown sugar, and honey. Then beat in the eggs, one at a time. Stir in the dry ingredients, chocolate bits, and walnuts.

Spread in a lightly greased 14-inch by 10-inch pan. Bake in a preheated 350° F. oven for 25 to 30 minutes. Cool and cut into bars.

Variations

Toffee Bars. Substitute 1 cup crushed toffee bars or toffee chips for the chocolate chips.

Peanut Butter Bars. Substitute 1 cup peanut butter chips for the chocolate chips.

Butterscotch Chewy Bars

1 cup whole wheat pastry flour
½ cup white flour
½ cup wheat germ
1 teaspoon baking soda
Dash salt
1½ cups bran flake cereal
½ cup brown sugar
¼ cup honey
¼ cup butter, at room temperature
¼ cup margarine, at room temperature
½ cup peanut butter
2 eggs
¼ cup nonfat dry milk powder
1 teaspoon vanilla extract
⅓ cup milk
1 cup butterscotch bits

These are overwhelmingly popular in my house. They are moist and hearty and nourishing, perfect in the school lunch.

Combine the flours, wheat germ, baking soda, salt, and bran flakes.

Cream the sugar, honey, butter, margarine, and peanut butter until light; beat in the eggs, dry milk, and vanilla. Add the dry ingredients alternately with the milk. Stir in the butterscotch bits.

Spread evenly in a lightly greased 14-inch by 10-inch pan. Bake in a preheated 350° F. oven for 20 to 25 minutes. Cut into bars while warm.

4
REFRIGERATOR COOKIES

These cookies are also known as sliced or icebox cookies. The dough is stiff; it must be chilled in the refrigerator until it is firm, so that it can be cut in slices as even and thin as possible. The real advantage of refrigerator cookies is that the dough can be kept on hand for a long time (at least 8 to 10 days when well wrapped and chilled), and the cookies can be sliced and baked when needed. The dough also freezes very well. And any of these doughs can be rolled out and cut in shapes if desired.

Refrigerator cookies are crisp, buttery, and subtle in flavor. Because they are thin, one batch goes a long way. And because of their crispness, they are more fragile than bars and most drop cookies and thus do not travel so well.

The easiest way to chill these cookies is to form the dough into a roll, the size of which you can decide yourself. Then tightly wrap the rolls in plastic wrap or aluminum foil and refrigerate until firm. Empty 6-ounce frozen fruit juice contain-ers make excellent storage forms for this dough, and the cookies come out as perfect circles. Also good for storage are ½-pint cream or milk cartons; open the top, pack the dough in tightly, and refrigerate until firm. Then carefully peel away the carton, and with a sharp knife slice the dough in ⅛-inch squares. Cut each square into 4 squares or cut on the diagonal to make triangles.

Vanilla Nut Cookies

1 cup whole wheat pastry flour
½ cup white flour
1½ teaspoons baking powder
¼ teaspoon salt
½ cup wheat germ
½ cup butter, at room temperature
½ cup brown sugar
¼ cup white sugar
¼ cup dry milk powder
1 egg
1 teaspoon vanilla extract
1 cup finely chopped or ground nuts
(walnuts, pecans, almonds, filberts)

Sift the flours with the baking powder and salt. Stir in the wheat germ and set aside.

Cream the butter until light and then gradually beat in the sugars and dry milk. Add the egg and vanilla and continue beating until very light and fluffy. Then stir in half the flour mixture. Gently mix in the remaining flour with your hands, forming a stiff dough. Add the nuts, mixing well.

Shape the dough into two rolls or pack into containers and refrigerate until firm—about 8 hours or overnight.

With a sharp knife, slice the dough in ⅛-inch slices. Place on lightly greased cookie sheets and bake in a preheated 375° F. oven for 8 to 10 minutes, or until lightly browned.

Be sure to tightly wrap whatever dough you don't use and store in the refrigerator.

Peanut Butter Pinwheels

Dough

½ **cup whole wheat pastry flour**
½ **cup white flour**
1 **teaspoon baking powder**
¼ **teaspoon salt**
½ **cup butter, at room temperature**
½ **cup peanut butter**
½ **cup brown sugar**
¼ **cup honey**
1 **egg**
1 **teaspoon vanilla extract**
1 **cup rolled oats**

Filling

1 **cup chopped dates**
¼ **cup honey**
⅓ **cup water**
2 **teaspoons grated lemon rind**
½ **cup finely chopped walnuts**

Refrigerator cookies can be made in many designs by combining doughs of different flavors and colors. And you can make cookies as pinwheels, with varied and interesting fillings.

To prepare the dough, sift together the flours, baking powder, and salt.

Cream together the butter, peanut butter, brown sugar, and honey until light and fluffy. Beat in the egg and vanilla until smooth. Add the flour mixture, stirring until well combined, then stir in the rolled oats. Refrigerate for 30 minutes.

Meanwhile, prepare the filling by cooking the dates, honey, and water in a small saucepan over medium heat, stirring, until the mixture thickens—about 5 minutes. Cool and stir in the lemon rind and nuts. Cool completely.

Divide the dough in half. On a lightly floured surface, roll each half into a rectangle about 8 inches by 10 inches. Spread each rectangle with half the date-nut mixture. From the long side, roll each, jelly-roll fashion. Gently press the edges and ends to seal.

Wrap separately, and place seam side down on a cookie sheet. Refrigerate until firm, about 8 hours. Then slice and place, about 1 inch apart, on lightly greased cookie sheets. Bake in a preheated 375° F. oven for 10 to 12 minutes or until golden.

Variation

Fig Pinwheels. Prepare the filling as given for Fig Bars (page 61). The filling should be thick. Cool it completely and substitute it for the date-nut filling.

Spice Cookies

½ cup butter, at room temperature
½ cup brown sugar
1 cup whole wheat pastry flour
¼ teaspoon baking soda
⅛ teaspoon salt
1 teaspoon cinnamon
¼ teaspoon cloves
¼ teaspoon nutmeg
½ cup wheat germ
¼ cup dry milk powder
2 tablespoons yogurt
½ cup chopped walnuts or almonds

This recipe makes a very soft dough that should be packed tightly in containers and chilled well. The cookie is crisp and has a lovely spice taste.

Cream together the butter and sugar until fluffy.

Sift together the flour, baking soda, salt, and spices; stir in the wheat germ and dry milk. Add the dry ingredients to the butter mixture along with the yogurt; then stir in the nuts. Chill overnight.

Arrange thin slices on lightly greased cookie sheets and press with a cookie press if you have one. Bake in a preheated 375° F. oven for 10 minutes. Watch the cookies as they burn easily.

Fruit Spritz

2 cups whole wheat pastry flour
2 cups white flour
1 teaspoon baking powder
Dash salt
½ cup rolled oats
½ cup butter, at room temperature
½ cup margarine, at room temperature
½ cup white sugar
¼ cup light honey
1 egg
2 tablespoons orange (or pineapple-orange) juice concentrate, thawed
¼ cup nonfat dry milk powder

Spritz are very popular cookies in Germany and Holland. This version has the added zest of fruit juice. You can shape this dough in rolls and slice it, or use a cookie press.

Sift together the flours, baking powder, and salt. Stir in the rolled oats and set aside.

Cream together the butter, margarine, sugar, and honey until light and fluffy. Beat in the egg, juice concentrate, and dry milk. Blend in the flour, one quarter at a time, making a stiff dough. Chill thoroughly.

Slice in ⅛-inch slices or put the dough through a cookie press. Arrange the cookies on lightly greased cookie sheets. Bake in a preheated 375° F. oven for about 10 minutes, until firm but not brown.

Sherry Thins

½ cup butter, at room temperature
¼ cup margarine, at room temperature
½ cup white sugar
¼ cup honey
1 egg
½ cup nonfat dry milk powder
2 cups whole wheat pastry flour
½ cup white flour
2 teaspoons baking powder
1 teaspoon nutmeg
½ teaspoon salt
½ cup wheat germ
⅓ cup cream sherry
1 egg white, slightly beaten
Grated almonds

These cookies are part of our Christmas each year. They are excellent with eggnog or a glass of crisp white wine.

Cream together the butter, margarine, sugar, and honey until light. Beat in the egg and dry milk until smooth.

Sift together the flours, baking powder, nutmeg, and salt. Stir in the wheat germ and add to the butter mixture alternately with the sherry. Shape into rolls and chill thoroughly.

Slice thin cookies from the roll, brush the tops with the egg white, and sprinkle with the almonds. Place on lightly greased cookie sheets and bake in a preheated 400° F. oven for 8 to 10 minutes.

Lemon and Cream Cheese Cookies

⅓ cup honey
⅓ cup oil
4 ounces cream cheese, at room temperature
1 cup whole wheat pastry flour
2 tablespoons wheat germ
¼ teaspoon salt
2 tablespoons lemon juice
1 teaspoon grated lemon rind
¼ cup poppy seeds

You can use chopped sunflower seeds instead of poppy seeds in these cookies if you prefer them. The combination of the cream cheese and poppy seeds is special, however.

Blend the honey, oil, and cream cheese (you can use half farmer cheese, ricotta, or well-drained creamed cottage cheese, if you like). Stir in the remaining ingredients in the order given. Shape the dough into rolls and chill.

Cut into thin slices and place on lightly greased cookie sheets. Bake in a preheated 400° F. oven for 5 to 8 minutes.

Rye Honey Crisps

1½ cups honey
2 tablespoons oil
1 cup rye flour
1 cup whole wheat pastry flour
1 teaspoon ginger
¼ teaspoon cloves
1 tablespoon fruit juice
½ teaspoon crushed anise seeds

The combined flavors of the rye flour, honey, and anise seeds make these cookies very unusual. They are quite dry and particularly good with applesauce or chilled mixed fruit.

Heat the honey to a boil and stir in the oil.

Sift the flours into a warm skillet over low heat, stirring constantly so they do not brown. Add the spices and mix quickly. Rapidly stir part of the flour into the hot honey. Add the rest of the flour with the fruit juice and anise seeds and stir hard until the dough comes off the spoon easily. Shape into long rolls and chill.

Cut the dough in ¼-inch slices and place on lightly greased cookie sheets. Bake in a preheated 325° F. oven for about 20 minutes, or until light brown.

5
ROLLED COOKIES

These cookies are made from dough stiff enough to roll thin. Thorough chilling of the dough is essential to successful rolled cookies. If the dough is not cool enough, it will need flour so that it doesn't stick. The more flour, the less tender are the cookies. It is best to remove from the refrigerator and roll out a small amount of dough at one time, so as to handle the dough as little as possible.

Roll out the dough on a lightly floured board, and use a pastry cover over the rolling pin if you have one. Cut the cookies as close together as possible; rerolling the dough will give you less tender cookies. Quick shapes can be made by cutting the dough in squares, rectangles, and triangles with a sharp knife.

Start a collection of interesting cookie cutters. We all have favorite shapes, suitable for special occasions. You can design your own by tracing what you like on stiff cardboard and cutting it out. Then place this pattern on the dough and cut around it with a sharp knife. All these cookies lend themselves to many kinds of decoration with fancy sugars and colored icings.

Lemon Cookies

½ cup honey
½ cup oil
4 tablespoons freshly grated lemon rind
2 tablespoons freshly grated orange rind
1 tablespoon lemon juice
1 egg, beaten
2 cups whole wheat pastry flour
½ cup white flour
¼ cup wheat germ
¼ cup oat bran
1 egg white, lightly beaten
¼ cup toasted soy grits

Blend the honey and oil. Combine with the grated rinds and lemon juice. Beat in the egg and then stir in the flours, wheat germ, oat bran, and dry milk. Chill the dough thoroughly.

Roll out the dough and cut into rounds or any desired shapes. Arrange on lightly greased cookie sheets. Brush the tops with the egg white and sprinkle with the soy grits. Bake in a preheated 350° F. oven until light brown, about 10 minutes.

Variation

Lemon Nut Cookies. Stir in 1 teaspoon nutmeg with the dry ingredients. Sprinkle with ground pecans or filberts instead of the soy grits.

English Raisin Cookies

2 cups whole wheat pastry flour
1 cup white flour
½ teaspoon baking soda
½ teaspoon salt
1 teaspoon cinnamon
1 teaspoon nutmeg
½ cup rolled oats
½ cup butter, at room temperature
½ cup light brown sugar
¼ cup light molasses
2 eggs
½ cup sour cream or yogurt
1 cup finely chopped raisins or currants

These cookies are traditionally part of the afternoon tea. If you don't like diamond shapes, try cutting them with a round or scalloped cutter.

Sift together the flours with the baking soda, salt, and spices. Stir in the rolled oats and set aside.

Cream together the butter, sugar, molasses, and eggs until light and fluffy. Add the sour cream and raisins and then, gradually, the flour mixture. Stir well to blend. Wrap the dough well and refrigerate for at least 1 hour.

Divide the dough into 4 parts and keep refrigerated until you are ready to roll out. Roll the dough, one part at a time, into a 14-inch by 12-inch rectangle. With a sharp knife, cut the dough on the diagonal to make diamond shapes, or cut into 18 bars.

Place 1½ inches apart on lightly greased cookie sheets. Reroll the trimmings and recut. Bake in a preheated 375° F. oven for 8 to 10 minutes, or until golden brown.

Variation

English Nut Cookies. Omit the cinnamon and increase the nutmeg to 1½ teaspoons. When rolling out the rectangles, sprinkle the dough with ½ cup finely chopped walnuts and press the nuts in with the rolling pin. Cut and bake as above.

Honey Hearts

1 cup honey
3 tablespoons butter
1 tablespoon oil
2 cups whole wheat pastry flour
2 cups white flour
1 teaspoon baking soda
1 teaspoon cinnamon
½ teaspoon nutmeg
½ cup wheat germ
2 eggs
½ cup ground almonds
⅓ cup finely chopped citron
1 tablespoon grated lemon rind
Simple Glaze (page 118) or red sugar or
    marzipan and candied violets or semi-
    sweet chocolate squares (optional)

I make these cookies for Valentine's Day each year. The dough can be cut into large hearts, which can then be decorated most beautifully. The cookies travel well and will keep for a long time in the refrigerator.

Heat the honey, butter, and oil in a small saucepan just until the mixture comes to a boil. Cool to lukewarm.

Sift together flours with the baking soda and spices and stir in the wheat germ; set aside.

Beat the eggs until light and then gradually beat in the honey mixture. Stir in the almonds, citron, and lemon rind. Gradually blend in the flour mixture to make a very stiff dough. Wrap tightly and refrigerate overnight.

Roll out the dough, one quarter at a

time, to a thickness of ¼ inch. Cut into desired shapes and arrange on lightly greased cookie sheets. Bake in a preheated 350° F. oven for 10 minutes or until light brown.

Cool completely and then glaze or decorate as desired. The cookies can also be covered with a chocolate glaze made by melting semisweet chocolate squares or bits. The chocolate makes a good background for writing sweet messages in pink frosting.

Christmas Sugar Cookies

1½ cups white flour
½ cup whole wheat pastry flour
1½ teaspoons baking powder
¼ teaspoon salt
½ cup butter, at room temperature
⅓ cup white sugar
⅓ cup honey
1 egg
¼ cup nonfat dry milk powder
½ teaspoon vanilla extract
½ teaspoon almond extract
1 tablespoon light cream

This recipe has been part of our Christmas tradition for as long as I can remember. Cutting out and decorating the cookies has been the source of great fun and has brought out rather amazing creativity. You can frost and decorate the baked cookies after they are cooled (use Simple Glaze, page 118, Butter Cream Frosting, page 115, or Honey Glaze, page 117). But we usually press colored sugars into the cookies before baking.

Sift the flours together and measure out 1½ cups; resift this with the baking powder and salt.

Cream the butter with the sugar and honey until fluffy; beat in the egg, dry milk, vanilla, almond extract, and cream. Stir in the remaining flour mixture until the dough is just blended. Chill thoroughly.

Roll out the dough ⅛ inch thick, working with a small amount of dough at a time. Cut with floured cutters to desired shapes and decorate. Place on lightly greased cookie sheets and bake in a preheated 375° F. oven for 5 to 8 minutes. Watch the cookies carefully as they can get too brown very quickly.

Ginger Cookies

⬡♡⬡⬡⬡♡⬡♡⬡♡⬡♡⬡♡⬡♡⬡♡⬡♡⬡♡⬡♡⬡♡⬡♡⬡♡⬡♡⬡♡⬡♡⬡♡⬡♡

⅓ **cup brown sugar**
⅓ **cup molasses**
1 teaspoon ginger
¼ **teaspoon cinnamon**
¼ **teaspoon cloves**
2 teaspoons baking soda
⅓ **cup butter**
1 egg
1½ cups whole wheat pastry flour
½ **cup white flour**
½ **cup wheat germ**

Here is the dark and spicy version for Christmas cookies and gingerbread men.

Combine the sugar, molasses, and spices in a large saucepan; bring to a boil and then remove from the heat. Stir in the baking soda and butter, stirring until the mixture thickens and the butter melts. Add the egg and beat vigorously. Finally stir in the flours and wheat germ until well combined. Refrigerate the dough until firm.

Cut the dough into 4 parts and roll out each part about ⅛ inch thick. Cut into desired shapes and arrange on lightly greased cookie sheets. Bake in a preheated 350° F. oven for 5 to 6 minutes.

6
UNBAKED COOKIES

Here are some ideas for cookies that require no baking. Sometimes, when the weather has been hot for days on end, it is helpful and very pleasant to be able to make cookies without heating up the kitchen with the oven. In some cases, you don't even need to cook anything at all. Also, unbaked cookies are a real time saver and often make the quickest treat of all. Many of the recipes in this chapter can be easily made by children.

Because no baking is required, the recipes generally rely upon ready-to-eat dried cereals, many of which are heavily fortified with vitamins and minerals. Do avoid the heavily sugared commercial cereals. I find that most commercial granolas are good for cookies; if they are very sweet, use less sweetening in the cookie mixture. Feel free to substitute cereals in these recipes. What is important is that you use what you have on hand and like yourself.

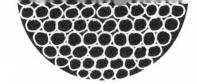

Honey Bites

3 tablespoons butter
2 tablespoons margarine
3 tablespoons milk
¼ cup white flour
¼ cup toasted wheat germ
2 tablespoons nonfat dry milk powder
¼ teaspoon salt
½ cup light honey
1 teaspoon vanilla extract
2 cups flaked coconut
2 cups crisp rice cereal

These crunchy balls have a wonderful taste of honey. If you prefer to use puffed wheat cereal, be sure it is crisp.

In a large saucepan, melt the butter and margarine. Stir in the milk, flour, wheat germ, dry milk, salt, and honey. Cook over medium heat, stirring constantly, until the mixture leaves the sides of the pan and forms a ball. Remove from the heat.

Stir in the vanilla, 1½ cups of the coconut, and the cereal. Shape into balls and roll the balls in the remaining ½ cup coconut. Store in the refrigerator.

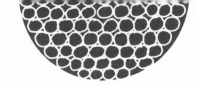

Cereal Date Balls

2 tablespoons butter
1½ cups chopped dates
¼ cup brown sugar
2 eggs, beaten
¼ teaspoon salt
2½ cups crisp rice cereal or cereal flakes
½ cup chopped walnuts
½ teaspoon vanilla extract
Coconut

These are among the best cookies of all time. They are sticky to make but provide fun for the children and are well worth the extra bother. Do use crisp brown rice cereal if possible.

Melt the butter in a heavy frying pan. Add the dates, sugar, eggs, and salt. Cook for about 10 minutes over very low heat, stirring constantly, until the mixture gets very bubbly. Remove from the heat and cool somewhat.

Add the cereal (if you use flakes, crush them a little first), nuts, and vanilla. Use spoons dipped in cold water to shape the dough into balls; then roll the balls in the coconut. Or you can drop teaspoons of the batter into the coconut and roll the balls with your fingers. In either case, press the balls firmly. Store refrigerated.

Variation

Orange Cereal Balls. Stir 2 tablespoons orange marmalade and 1 tablespoon grated orange rind into the date-egg mixture while it is cooking. Increase the cereal to 3 cups.

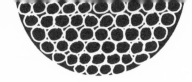

Maple Creamy Cereal Balls

¾ cup dried apricots
½ cup chopped pecans
¼ cup chopped raisins
¼ cup toasted flaked coconut
½ cup maple syrup
1 package (8 ounces) cream cheese
½ teaspoon vanilla extract
2½ cups puffed millet, rice, or wheat cereal

These balls have the lovely flavor of maple syrup and a creamy consistency as well. They are quite rich, so make them small.

Plump the apricots by pouring boiling water over them; let them stand for several minutes. Then drain and chop fine or puree in a processor. Mix with the pecans, raisins, and coconut. Set aside.

Combine the maple syrup, cream cheese, and vanilla until well blended. Stir in the fruits and nuts along with the cereal. Mix well. Form into small balls and chill thoroughly. Store in the refrigerator.

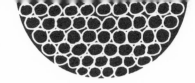

Peanut Butter Balls

1 cup peanut butter
⅓ cup nonfat dry milk powder
¼ cup honey
¼ cup toasted sesame seeds
¼ cup raisins
¼ cup graham cracker crumbs
½ cup flaked coconut

These, as well as the Moon Balls and Coconut Fruit Balls that follow, provide splendid opportunities for small children to prepare wholesome and delicious snacks. With a little guidance, the children can do it all themselves.

Mix the ingredients in the order given, saving some of the coconut. Roll into balls, using the remaining coconut for a coating. Chill thoroughly and store in a cool place.

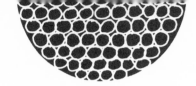

Moon Balls

1 cup nonfat dry milk powder
½ cup honey
½ cup peanut butter
½ cup granola, crushed fine
Toasted flaked coconut (optional)

These are very simple and very easy to make.

Mix the dry milk, honey, and peanut butter together until well blended. Chill. Form the dough into balls and roll in the granola. Or you can blend in the granola, form into balls, and roll them in toasted flaked coconut. Store in the refrigerator.

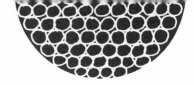

Coconut Fruit Balls

½ cup finely chopped dried apricots
¼ cup honey or light molasses
¼ cup brown sugar
3 tablespoons butter
2 tablespoons margarine
2 cups granola with nuts
1 cup flaked coconut
2 tablespoons toasted sesame seeds

These are crunchy and filled with good fruit, coconut, and seeds. You can use other dried fruits—dates, raisins, pineapple are good—or a combination of fruits. If you use sweeter fruit, then reduce the amount of brown sugar.

Combine the apricots, honey, sugar, butter, and margarine in a large saucepan. Bring the mixture to a boil. Reduce the heat and simmer for 5 minutes, stirring occasionally. Remove from the heat and stir in the granola, coconut, and sesame seeds. Cool for 15 minutes. Shape into balls and store in the refrigerator.

Variation

Just Right Fruit Balls. Substitute 2 cups of Kellogg's Just Right cereal (the variety with fruit and nuts) for the granola.

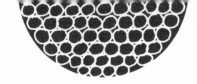

Easy Granola Bars

2 tablespoons butter
2 tablespoons margarine
2 tablespoons brown sugar
¼ cup honey
3 tablespoons peanut butter
2 tablespoons nonfat dry milk powder
2 tablespoons toasted sesame seeds
4 cups Kellogg's Just Right cereal
⅓ cup raisins

I generally make these with Kellogg's Just Right cereal (the fruit and nut variety), but you can substitute commercial granola with fruit and nuts for part or all of it. These are the quickest and most delicious and nutritious bars I can think of.

Combine the butter, margarine, brown sugar, and honey in a large saucepan. Bring to a full boil and boil for 1 minute, stirring constantly. Be careful not to overcook. Remove from the heat immediately and stir in the remaining ingredients in the order given. Press this mixture very firmly into a 9-inch square pan. Let stand for 30 minutes and then cut into bars.

Variation

Easy Cereal Bars. Substitute Kellogg's Nutri-Grain with Almonds, Raisin Bran, or Special K for the Just Right cereal and increase the brown sugar to ¼ cup. Add additional raisins and nuts if desired.

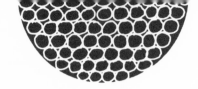

Oatmeal Fudgies

1 cup honey
½ cup milk
¼ cup butter
¼ cup oil
¼ cup nonfat dry milk powder
5 tablespoons cocoa
3 cups rolled oats (quick cooking, if possible)
1 teaspoon vanilla extract
¼ cup chopped walnuts

These are rich and delicious and quickly made.

Combine the honey, milk, butter, and oil in a large saucepan. Bring to a boil over medium heat, stirring constantly. Remove from the heat and stir in the dry milk and cocoa until well blended. Then gradually add the rolled oats, vanilla, and nuts, blending well. Drop by the tablespoon onto waxed paper and allow to cool overnight.

Variation

Carob Oatmeal Fudgies. Substitute 6 tablespoons carob powder for the cocoa, reduce the vanilla to ½ teaspoon, and add ½ teaspoon almond extract.

7
GLAZES AND FROSTINGS

Most cookies don't need anything added to their essential goodness. A few, however, are better with a frosting or glaze. Feel free to add or omit as you wish. Remember that these toppings add extra sweetness and usually some butter. Remember, too, that frostings are somewhat messy, and frosted cookies don't store and travel very easily.

Do use freshly squeezed orange and lemon juice as well as freshly grated orange and lemon rind in these recipes. You will not regret the extra effort.

Orange Glaze

½ cup 10X sugar
2 tablespoons honey
1 teaspoon grated orange rind
Approximately 1 tablespoon orange juice

Blend the sugar, honey, and orange rind until smooth. Gradually add enough orange juice to make a spreading consistency.

Cran-Orange Glaze

1 cup 10X sugar
2 tablespoons honey
1 tablespoon ground fresh or frozen
    cranberries or whole berry sauce
1 teaspoon grated orange rind
Orange juice (optional)

Blend the sugar and honey with the cranberries and the orange rind. If the mixture is too thin, stir in more sugar. If too thick, add a very small amount of orange juice.

Lemon Frosting

½ cup honey
Grated rind of 1 lemon
2 teaspoons lemon juice
¾ cup nonfat dry milk powder
10X sugar (optional)

Measure the honey, lemon rind, and lemon juice into the blender and whirl for several seconds. Add the dry milk and blend for a minute, or until very smooth. If too thin, add a small amount of 10X sugar. Let this stand for 30 minutes before using.

Lemon Glaze

3 tablespoons milk
2 tablespoons butter
¼ cup nonfat dry milk powder
2 tablespoons honey
1½ cups 10X sugar
1 teaspoon grated lemon rind
Approximately 3 tablespoons lemon juice

Heat the milk and the butter in a saucepan. Stir in the dry milk until smooth, then blend in the honey. Measure the 10X sugar into a bowl. Add the hot liquid and stir until smooth. Then blend in the lemon rind and enough lemon juice to make a spreading consistency.

Butter Cream Frosting

1 cup 10X sugar
1 tablespoon butter, at room temperature
2 tablespoons light cream or milk
¼ teaspoon vanilla extract

Beat or stir these ingredients until smooth.

Butter Frosting

⅓ **cup butter**
⅓ **cup honey**
1 teaspoon lemon juice

Cream the butter until light and fluffy. Slowly blend in the honey and lemon juice. Chill before spreading.

Honey Glaze

½ **cup honey**
1 cup nonfat dry milk powder
¼ **teaspoon vanilla extract**
Dash salt

Measure the honey into the blender and turn it on. Slowly add the milk powder, a little at a time, until thick. Blend in the vanilla and salt and whirl until smooth. Let this stand for about 30 minutes before using.

Simple Glaze

1 cup 10X sugar
½ cup honey
1 teaspoon butter
Whole milk

Measure the sugar into a bowl. Beat in the honey, butter, and enough milk to make a rather thin icing.

Cream Cheese Frosting

1 small package (3 ounces) cream cheese,
   at room temperature
1 cup 10X sugar
3 tablespoons honey or maple syrup

You can substitute ricotta for the cream cheese, if you like. Add 1 tablespoon soft butter to the frosting if you do so.

Beat the cream cheese until fluffy. Add the sugar alternately with the honey and beat until smooth. If the mixture is too thick, add more honey.

Appendix

Here is a comparison of the nutrients in many of the ingredients used in this book. (Sources: *Nutritive Value of Foods*, USDA Home and Garden Bulletin Number 72, and *Laurel's Kitchen*, Robertson et. al., Bantam, 1978.)

Food	Amt.	Cal.	Calcium /mg.	Iron /mg.	Potass. /mg.	Vit. A /I.U.	Thiam. /mg.	Rib. /mg.	Niacin /mg.	Vit. C /mg.
Nonfat dry milk	1 cup	245	837	.2	1,160	1,610	.28	1.19	.6	4
Yogurt (lowfat)	8 oz.	145	415	.2	531	150	.08	.49	.3	2
Eggs	1	80	28	1.0	65	260	.004	.15	Tr.	0
Apples	1	80	10	.2	159	70	.02	.02	.1	8
Apricots, dried	1 cup	310	59	6.1	1,791	9,410	.01	.20	3.9	3
Banana	1	105	7	.4	451	90	.05	.11	.6	10
Dates (chopped)	1 cup	490	57	2.0	1,161	40	.07	.08	1.8	0
Prunes	5 large	115	25	1.2	365	970	.04	.08	1.0	2
Raisins	1 cup	145	71	3.0	1,089	10	.23	.13	1.2	5
Rolled oats	1 cup	145	19	1.6	131	40	.26	.05	.3	0
All-Bran cereal	⅓ cup	70	23	4.5	350	1,250	.37	.43	5.0	15
Corn flakes (Kellogg's)	1¼ cups	110	1	1.8	26	1,250	.37	.43	5.0	15
Grape-Nuts cereal	¼ cup	110	11	1.2	95	1,250	.37	.43	5.0	15
Product 19 cereal	¾ cup	110	3	18.0	44	5,000	1.50	1.70	20.0	60

Food	Amt.	Cal.	Calcium /mg.	Iron /mg.	Potass. /mg.	Vit. A /I.U.	Thiam. /mg.	Rib. /mg.	Niacin /mg.	Vit. C /mg.
Special K cereal	1⅓ cups	110	8	4.5	49	1,250	.37	.43	5.0	15
Total cereal	1 cup	100	48	18.0	106	5,000	1.50	1.70	20.0	60
All-purpose flour (enriched)	1 cup	125	18	5.1	109	0	.73	.46	6.1	0
Whole wheat	1 cup	400	49	5.2	444	0	.66	.14	5.2	0
Soy flour (defatted)	1 cup	326	270	11.0	1800	40	1.10	.34	2.6	0
Wheat bran	1 cup	111	62	7.7	580	0	.37	.18	11.0	0
Wheat germ	1 cup	298	59	7.7	680	0	1.60	.56	3.4	0
Almonds, slivered	1 cup	795	359	4.9	988	0	.28	1.05	4.5	1
Coconut, shredded	1 cup	285	11	1.9	285	0	.05	.02	.4	3
Peanuts, dry roasted	1 oz.	170	20	1.0	169	Tr.	.06	.06	1.3	0
Peanut butter	1 tbl.	95	5	.3	110	0	.02	.02	2.2	0
Pecan halves	1 cup	720	314	2.3	423	140	.92	.14	1.0	2
Brown sugar	1 cup	820	187	4.8	757	0	0.2	.07	.2	0
White sugar	1 cup	770	3	.1	7	0	0.00	0.0	0	
Molasses, blackstrap	2 tbl.	85	274	10.1	1.171	0	.04	.08	.8	0
Honey	1 cup	1,030	17	1.7	173	0	.02	.14	1.0	3

INDEX